ACKNOWLED

The production of this title was only possible assistance and patience of many fine people that I am lucky enough to call my friends.

— Tom Bolfert, Mike Millay and the patient archivists and restoration experts at Harley-Davidson's history department.

— Ed Rich and his famous collection at the American Classic Motorcycle Co., Asheboro, North Carolina.

— John Archaki and his private menagerie of perfect machines.

— Lee Mattes, Dave Reuland, Terry Grimes, Ken Weinstein and the entire staff at Heritage Harley-Davidson, Lisle, Illinois.

ACKNOWLEDGMENTS

— Dave Kiesow, Bob Maxant and the energetic gang at Illinois Harley-Davidson, Berwyn, Illinois.

— Jim Kersting, his family and the talented team at Kersting's Harley-Davidson & Cycle Center, North Judson, Indiana.

— John Parham, Jeff Carstensen and the tireless crew at the National Motorcycle Museum, Anamosa, Iowa.

— Joyce Harlan at Walters Brothers Harley-Davidson, Peoria, Illinois.

— Dale Walksler, and his world-class Wheels Through Time Museum, Maggie Valley, North Carolina.

INTRODUCTION

With little more than a dream and some wide-eyed enthusiasm, two young men in Milwaukee designed and built a simple motorcycle in 1903. Using other machines of the period for guidance, they crafted their own motor and frame. The resulting machine was fairly simple, but in line with other cycles being built at the time. Most of the other builders would disappear as quickly as they began, but the Harley-Davidson brand endured.

More than a century later, Harley-Davidson remains America's motorcycle brand. Assembled at several facilities in the U.S., the company stands for American pride and ingenuity. Sales and popularity have extended world wide, and the Harley-Davidson name is recognized at every corner of the known universe.

The models have changed with the times, but their true nature remains unaltered.

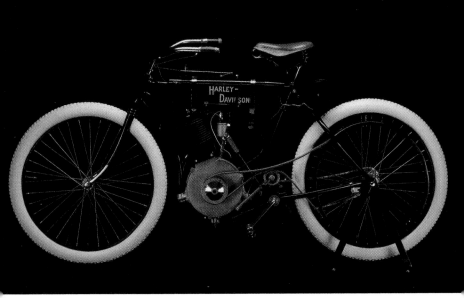

HARLEY-DAVIDSON
FIELD GUIDE

Doug Mitchel

ALL-AMERICAN BIKES 1903-2004

©2005 by KP Books
Published by

kp books
An Imprint of F+W Publications

700 East State Street • Iola, WI 54990-0001
715-445-2214 • 888-457-2873

Our toll-free number to place an order or obtain a free catalog is (800) 258-0929.

Library of Congress Catalog Number: 2004114242
ISBN: 0-87349-338-9

Designed by Kay Sanders
Edited by Brian Earnest
Printed in the United States of America

CONTENTS

CONTENTS

CONTENTS

To my friend Jennifer

1903 (SERIAL #1)

Built in a small wooden shed, serial number 1 was the machine that started it all. The simple motorcycle was the combination of existing hardware, fresh designs and the energetic dream of two men. Little did they know that more than 100 years later, machines bearing their names would still be in production, and adored by people all around the globe.

◆ The single cylinder motor displaced 24.74 inches and produced roughly 3 horsepower.

◆ A frame built by Merkel was used as a guideline for the chassis.

◆ Harley and Davidson initially planned on using a liquid-cooled motor, but the weight and complexity of such a design led them to the air-cooled motor instead.

1905 MODEL 1

"Production" of the 1905 Model 1 is rumored to have reached a total of 5 units, but record keeping was lax in the early days as the company focused on building machines, not keeping track of its efforts. Very few alterations were made in the first years of assembly.

◆ **The Model 1 remained the only version sold for 1905.**
◆ **A three-coil pillion helped to absorb the bumps before they reached the rider.**
◆ **A 1905 model was ridden to a new speed record at a local event by Perry E. Mack.**

Owner: Harley-Davidson Motor Company

The F-head motor was revised both inside and out for 1905. A 1/8-inch-larger bore bumped horsepower to a total of 3 1/4, and the displacement to 26.84 cubic inches. At the time, motorcycles were gaining in popularity with every passing day, helping the newfound Harley-Davidson company to flourish.

1907 MODEL 3

The 1907 Model 3's were not much different than the 1906 Model 2's they replaced, but sales remained brisk. The single-cylinder motor had revised mounting hardware, and the large cylindrical engine case was now assembled with eight bolts.

◆ **Production of the 1907 Model 3's reached 150 units.**
◆ **It cost the buyer $210 for every Model 3 they bought, but many were happy to pay the price.**
◆ **A twin-cylinder motor was attempted by Harley-Davidson, but results proved dismal.**

Owner: National Motorcycle Museum

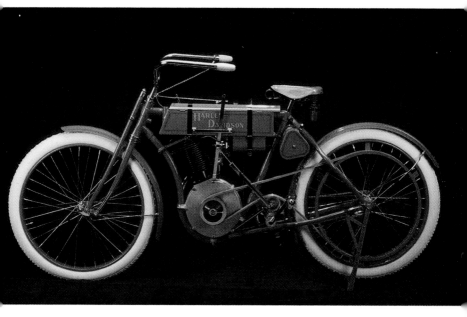

The left side of the Model 3 shows the belt drive and tension adjuster. The leather belt drive system would remain on Harley-Davidsons until the first chain appeared in 1913. The first twin-cylinder model would not be seen until 1911.

The standard method for mounting the flat-sided fuel tank to the frame was the pair of steel straps. This system begat the "strap tank" nickname to the early Harley models.

1909 MODEL 5D

1909 would mark the first year of a production V-twin motor from Harley-Davidson. An earlier attempt was made, but proved unsuccessful. Of the five models offered in 1909, only one, the 5D, was propelled by the newest motor. The 45-degree cylinder placement began H-D's longstanding application of that design formula.

◆ **The new twin-cylinder motor delivered 7 horsepower and displaced 53.68 cubic inches.**
◆ **A magneto ignition was another new feature used on the 1909 models.**
◆ **Trouble with the latest motor design forced its removal from the sales catalog the following year.**

Owner: Harley-Davidson Archives

The wide, flat leather drive belt remained the standard method of propulsion for 1909 Harley-Davidsons. Riding in wet conditions caused the belt to slip on the drive pulleys, and proved to be just one of the faults with this system.

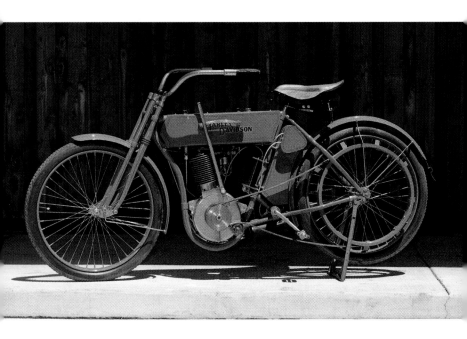

1910 MODEL 6

With the removal of the twin-cylinder option, the 1910 catalog showed only four variations of the single-lung models. The model 6 seen here rolls on 28-inch tires and wheels and is started with a battery ignition. Of course, pedal power was still the method employed to get things going, since the electric start option would not appear until 1965.

◆ The Model 6 outsold all other varieties of Harley in 1910 with 2,302 copies rolling off the sales floors.
◆ Both the Model 6 and 6B sold for $210 in 1910.
◆ Additional cooling fins were added to the motor to assist in keeping temperatures under control.

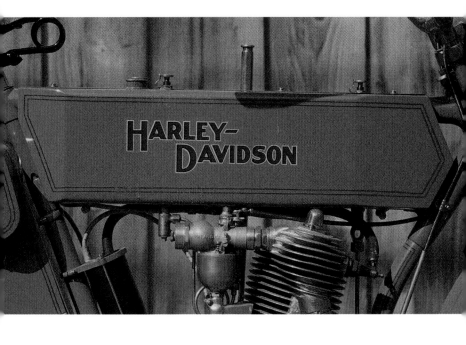

Fuel tanks would retain their slab-sided designs until metalworking became more flexible in the following years. From the very start, Harley-Davidsons utilized a high degree of detail in its pin striping and application of colors.

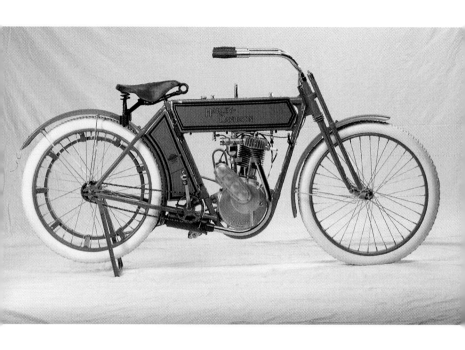

1911 MODEL 7A

Another version of the earlier V-twin motor would return for 1911, but the single-cylinder models retained the lion's share of production. The 7A featured 28-inch tires and wheels, as well as a magneto-fired ignition. Other variants rolled on 26-inch rubber and could be battery or magneto equipped.

◆ The 1911 Model 7 had a pair of 28-inch wheels and battery ignition.
◆ $250 would get you a choice of the 7A or 7C, while $225 earned you the 7 or 7C.
◆ The 1911 V-twin Model 7D carried an MSRP of $300.

Owner: National Motorcycle Museum

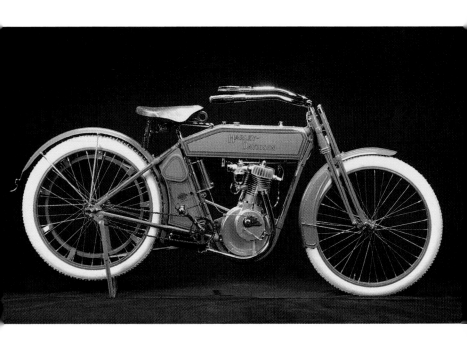

1912 MODEL 8

There were four variants of the 1912 single-cylinder models, and the Model 8 was fitted with a battery ignition. The same 30.16-cubic inch motor was found in the frame. The Model 8 was the least expensive machine Harley sold in 1908.

◆ Only $200 was required to ride home on your own Model 8 in 1912.

◆ The single-cylinder models were joined by a trio of twin-cylinder machines in the sales catalog.

◆ Two other single-cylinder models were fitted with magneto ignitions this year.

Owner: National Motorcycle Museum

1912 would be the final year of the belt drive as Harley adopted a chain for the final drive in 1913. With the change to chain drive, the belt-tensioner was also a thing of the past in 1913.

1914 BOARD TRACK RACER

With privateers racking up an impressive list of "wins" aboard Harley-Davidsons in 1911 and 1912, the factory decided to join the fray. This 1914 model is a factory-built machine designed specifically to attack the wooden ovals across the United States.

◆ This bike was powered by a 61-cubic inch V-twin "A" motor and equipped with only a tiny rear brake
◆ The short-coupled frame was fitted with a highly modified motor. Larger valves, intake and Schebler carburetor were teamed with improved cam timing.
◆ The long-distance race tank featured rivets that helped to hold the seams together.

Owner: Wheels Through Time Museum

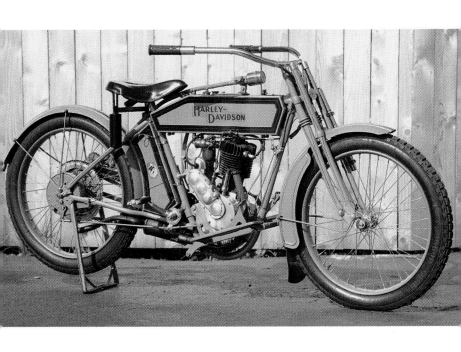

1914 MODEL 10C

Almost all of the 1914 models were finally driven by chain in place of the previous leather belt. The chain drive allowed for wet weather riding without the slippage often experienced with a belt. The 1914 Model 10A retained the belt drive, but all others had the latest chain.

◆ The Model 10C shifted through a two-speed hub on the rear wheel.
◆ There were three single-cylinder and three twin-cylinder models sold in 1914.
◆ The Model 10C sold for $245, and fewer than 900 units were purchased.

Owner: Dave Kiesow

1915 MODEL 11F

The 11F was positioned near the bottom of the Harley-Davidson product range for 1915, but outsold the next-best model by almost 3 to 1. The 60.34-cubic inch V-twin motor was mated to a three-speed gearbox, which gave the rider some flexibility to meet with changing conditions.

◆ 1915 was the last year before model designations matched their sales year.

◆ 9,855 sales of the 11F were recorded in 1915, each with a retail price of $275.

◆ The only V-twin model beneath the 11F was the 11E, and its sales barely broke 100 for the same year.

Owner: Bob Maxant

1916 MODEL 16F

The 1916 Harleys carried model designations matching the same year they were offered. The 16F was built with a magneto ignition and three-speed transmission. The F-head V-twin was still the power plant of choice, and the F model outsold all others in 1916.

◆ The fuel/oil tanks on the 1916 models were curvaceous in comparison to the previous boxy versions.

◆ In addition to their new contours, the tanks held two additional pints of fluid.

◆ Both the single and twin-cylinder machines rode with the same chassis.

Owner: Bob McClean

While the 1916 Model 16J was fitted with an electrical system, the 16F relied on a tank of gas for lighting. Both the head and taillights were illuminated by burning the gas stored in the handlebar-mounted reservoir. Needless to say, the output was hardly enough to light the roads at night, but it was better than having no lights at all.

1916 MODEL 16J

The 16J was still powered by the same 60.34-cubic inch V-twin as the rest of the 1916 twin-cylinder lineup, but it was purchased complete with an electrical system. This arrangement provided battery power for the ignition, as well as sending the signal to the head and taillights.

◆ H-D produced 5,898 Model 16Js for 1916. They carried a price tag of $295.

◆ Harleys came with wider-spaced front forks in 1916.

◆ Racing was still a big influence to H-D in 1916 and the company had two racing models — both F-head twins – in its lineup.

1917 MODEL 17C

The single-cylinder models were never big sellers when the V-twin delivered a healthier dose of power for only a few dollars more. The three-speed variant of the one-lung Harley, the 17C, still sold better than the single-speed variety. This example has been bridled with a rare wicker sidecar, adding a high degree of versatility.

◆ **The single-cylinder, F-head motor displaced 35 cubic inches.**
◆ **A handful more than 600 17C models were sold at $240 each.**
◆ **Lacking electrics, the 17C ran the lighting system via gas stored in a small auxiliary tank.**

Owner: Pete Bollenbach

1917 MODEL 17F

The three-speed, magneto-fired 17F was only outsold by the electrically fired 17J that year. A four-lobe cam layout was implemented into all F-head models in 1917, adding durability to the existing design. Both inlet and exhaust valve springs were now enclosed on the 1917 motors.

◆ The 17F was outsold only by the 17J in 1917. The main difference between the bikes was the electrical system.
◆ The 17F was delivered with no lighting at all. A gas-charged system could be added to the model.
◆ It required 275 American dollars to ride off with a new 17F in 1917.

Owner: National Motorcycle Museum

1919 MODEL 19J

The 1919 Model J was one of only four machines in the catalog for that year, and was powered by the same 60.34-cubic inch V-twin as two of the others. The F-head twin motor was widely accepted, and would see duty for many years to come in the Harley family of motorcycles. This example has been accessorized with a rear-mounted luggage rack and leather carrying bag.

◆ **For 1919, only the Sport model boasted a horizontally opposed twin motor.**
◆ **Nearly 10,000 copies of the Model J were sold in 1919.**
◆ **A post-war vacuum of imported motorcycles left Harley-Davidson as the market leader when peace was restored.**

Owner: Aaron Mohr

The F-Head V-twin motor had proven to be a reliable and fairly foolproof design as the years had moved along. A cam-actuated clutch replaced the previous work gear-actuated device on the 1919 models.

1919 MODEL WF

In a radical departure from their typical V-twin architecture, the 19WF, or Sport model, was motivated by a horizontally opposed mill. Displacing 35.64 cubic inches, the Sport's cylinders ran inline with the chassis. A trailing link front fork was also used for the first time, but sales of the bike were not what Harley had hoped for.

◆ **The displacement of the new motor was only marginally larger than the single-cylinder models.**
◆ **A total of 6 horsepower was available from the opposed twin motor.**
◆ **Despite the raft of new technology, only 753 19WF models were produced in 1919.**

Owner: Tom Baer

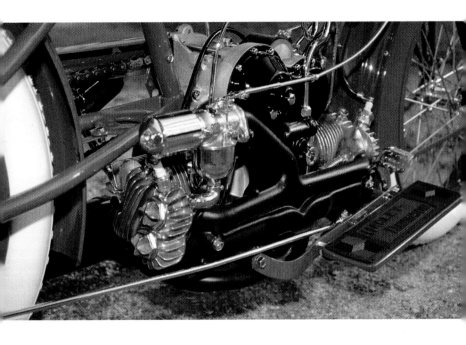

The new motor layout was compact on the Sport model and acted as a stressed member of the frame. Total displacement of both cylinders barely outsized that of the single-cylinder models, and horsepower was rated at a meager 6.

1920 MODEL 20J

Harley-Davidson found itself at the top of the heap once WWI had ended, and the company had plans to keep itself there. In an effort to produce smooth-running motors, compression plates were added as needed. These plates guaranteed equal compression in each cylinder, enhancing the overall operation of the V-twin mills.

◆ The Model 20J featured a three-speed gearbox and an electrical system.
◆ Despite it being the highest-priced model in 1920, the 20J outsold all other Harley models that year.
◆ 14,192 examples of the 20J were produced to meet with growing demand.

Owner: Henry Hardin Family

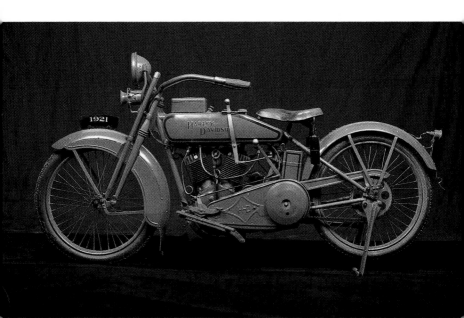

1921 MODEL 21J

The Model 21J was still motivated by the 60.34-cubic inch motor, but a larger 74-cubic inch variant was now being sold by Harley-Davidson. A variety of incremental changes were made to the Sixty-One models, and sales remained strong.

◆ Late in the model year, the Sixty-One motors were fitted with solid flywheels.
◆ Revisions to the fenders and fuel tank also separated the 1921 models from the previous editions.
◆ 4,526 Model 21Js were sold at $485 each, making them the top seller that year.

Owner: Harley-Davidson Archives

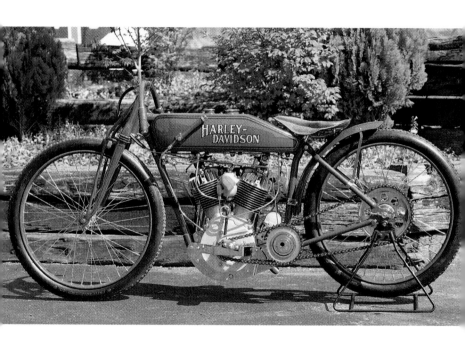

1922 MODEL JD BOARD TRACK RACER

By the time 1922 arrived, factory-supported board track racing was waning fast. Victories at the track seemed to matter less and less to retail sales, so it was only natural to pull the plug. Harley-Davidson's "Wrecking Crew" had achieved a high level of success throughout the years, and their machines were typically equipped as the one shown here.

◆ **No brakes, and very little suspension define board track machines.**
◆ **The steeply dropped handlebars kept the rider in a perfect tuck needed to aid in aerodynamics.**
◆ **The hard leather saddle was hardly comfortable, but board track racing was not the sport of comfort.**

Owner: Wheels Through Time Museum

1924 MODEL JE

The catalog for 1924 was expanded to 14 models, and
the JE ended up the winner in the sales race. Aluminum
pistons and an electrical system were two of the highlights
responsible for the strong customer demand.

◆ **The JE was still powered by the smaller "Sixty-One" motor, but now featured aluminum pistons.**
◆ **A total of 12 grease fittings could be used on the 1924 models to keep things properly lubed.**
◆ **A box-shaped muffler was part of the equipment in 1924 — the only year of this arrangement.**

1925 MODEL JES

For those riders who demanded a bit more utility from their Harleys, a sidecar could be added. The 1925 Model JES was trimmed with both an electrical system and specific sidecar gearing. A "Sixty-One" motor provided the required propulsion.

◆ **The model parade was whittled down to eight options in 1925.**
◆ **The electrical system and sidecar gearing were available for $315.**
◆ **Sidecar options were few and factory offerings even fewer. This Model LT hack was designed for use by one passenger and was included in Harley's sales literature that year.**

Owner: Illinois Harley-Davidson

1925 MODEL JD

For 1925, many changes were made to the looks and performance of the Harley team. The sleeker teardrop-shaped tanks and lower saddle height gave the Model JD a new profile. The battery position was now upright—another subtle styling cue.

◆ A 3-inch-lower seat height allowed smaller riders to join the riding fun.
◆ Aiding in comfort were the new handlebars, which reached back to greet the rider's hands.
◆ Four more grease fittings were added, providing a total of 16 lubrication points.

Owner: Kersting's Harley-Davidson

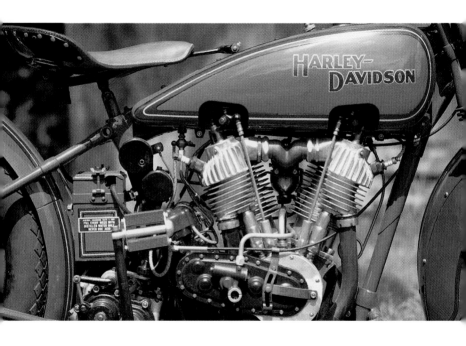

The newly shaped teardrop fuel tank featured cutouts for the valve train. The battery box was now positioned vertically instead of riding at a slightly canted angle.

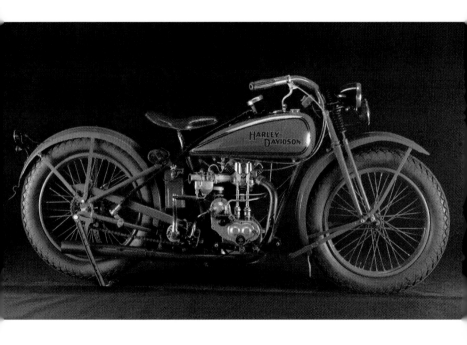

1926 MODEL BA "PEASHOOTER"

Harley-Davidson sold five different single-cylinder models in 1926, three of which featured overhead-valve motors. The BA seen here was the model that had an electrical system to power the head and taillights. The 26S was built for racing only and featured a magneto.

◆ The overhead-valve single displaced 21.35 cubic inches.
◆ All 1926 Harley gearboxes held three speeds within their cases.
◆ 515 BA models were sold at a cost of $275 each.

Owner: Bruce Linsday

The "Peashooter" bikes showcased overhead-valve motors and were fairly quick considering their small displacement. The AA, BA and S models all shared the same basic power plant, but the BA had an electrical system.

1927 MODEL JD

There were nine 1927 models offered, with four being powered by the twin-cylinder motors. The singles were first seen in 1926, and while popular, did not sell as well as the JD. The big 74-cubic inch engine delivered plenty of power and was gaining more reliability with every passing year.

◆ The new ignition fired without a distributor, eliminating wet weather troubles.
◆ All 1927 machines from Harley were fitted with three-speed gearboxes.
◆ Production of the JD reached 9,691 bikes, which was almost three times the next-best seller.

Fuel tanks on the 1927 models were still formed in the sleek teardrop shape with the scoop-out segments that allowed for the valve train's movements. The olive paint was offset by colorful pinstripe details. 1927 was the last year for the olive-painted crankcases. With nearly 9,700 units rolling out dealers' doors, the Model JD was the most popular bike in Harley's lineup.

1930 HILL CLIMBER

Hill climbing was a popular motor sport in the 1930s, and specially built machines were created to meet the challenge of this sport. This 1930 factory-built model featured unusual trailing-link front forks. Another detail was the angle of the floorboards. The angle seemed unnatural while on level ground, but fit the rider's posture perfectly on a steep ascent.

◆ **The tiny fuel tank held all the fuel the bike needed for a few quick runs, and didn't add a lot of excess weight.**

◆ **Many hill climb attempts were aided by a set of rear wheels chains, but they were not applied to this example.**

◆ **The motor of this 1930 climber functions with the use of specially designed overhead valves.**

Owner: Wheels Through Time Museum

To power the cycle up a steep incline, a 45-cubic inch motor was installed. The purpose-built machine featured overhead-valve cylinder heads for an extra dose of horsepower.

1931 VL POLICE

The 1931 Harley-Davidson family of motorcycles was mostly a repeat of the previous year, but minor changes were seen. Use of two-wheeled machines on police forces had become fairly common as early as the 1920s, and this 1931 VL was also pressed into official duty.

◆ Single headlights were again the common practice for Harley, and a 7-inch "John Brown Motolamp" was chosen for duty.
◆ Single tube mufflers were now used on the 45- and 74-inch models.
◆ Red warning lights, a hard-sided storage box and the fire extinguisher were commonly found on police duty cycles of the period.

1932 MODEL V

With the world's economy still gripped by depression, 1932 would not be a year of drastic change. The chain guard mounting points were altered to avoid a broken drive chain from getting jammed into the previous space. A fuel strainer helped to keep bits of debris from working their way into the fuel system.

◆ **The 1932 Model V was one of four Harleys powered by the 74-cubic inch motor that year.**
◆ **The Model V engine featured medium compression and shifted through three speeds.**
◆ **478 copies of the Model V were produced and sold for $320 each.**

Owner: Ray Schlee

1933 MODEL RL

With the American economy still in shambles, 1933 was not a year of overwhelming changes for Harley-Davidson. A new "Ride Control" option was added to provide an extra measure of comfort to both the rider and passenger. A pair of slotted steel plates on the front fork allowed the stiffness of the springs to be adjusted to suit the rider's needs.

◆ New tank graphics were applied in an effort to spruce up the existing models.
◆ The RL motor displaced 45 cubic inches and the gearbox provided a choice of three gears.
◆ 264 RLs were sold at a cost of $280 each in 1933.

Owner: Wheels Through Time Museum

1934 MODEL VLD

All 1934, twin-cylinder models from Harley received improved lubrication components to assist in engine longevity. The total loss system was still implemented, and an improved pump was employed. Frame augmentation resulted in a stouter platform for the remaining assembly.

◆ 1934 models were also fitted with newly shaped fenders in the front and rear.

◆ Two-tone paint schemes, upswept exhaust on the twins, and splashier tank graphics helped boost sales.

◆ 4,527 copies of the VLD were constructed for 1934, and they carried a retail price of $310.

Owner: Paul Ross

1934 MODEL VL

Since the 1920s, Harley-Davidsons had been pressed into municipal service with a variety of police departments. Compared to today's two-wheeled patrol units, the 1934 editions were sparsely equipped with warning lights or departmental markings.

1935 MODEL VLD

1935 would be a year of only nominal changes for the Harley-Davidson lineup. With the pending release of the all-new Knucklehead motor in 1936, the company was busy looking ahead. The flathead motors of 1935 would displace either 45, 74 or 80 cubic inches, depending on the model. The large 80-inch models were not seen until later in the model year.

◆ The VLD displaced 74 cubic inches and was mated to a three-speed gearbox.
◆ Although not the cheapest 1935 model ($320), the VLD was the top seller that year.
◆ New Lynite pistons rode in straight-bore cylinders, a big change from the tapered wall versions seen in 1934.

Owner: Wheels Through Time Museum

1936 MODEL EL

Up until now, the Harley catalog had been filled with a wide variety of machines powered by F-head and Flathead motors. The all-new Knucklehead was a great leap forward in technology and power. The overhead-valve mill was a first for Harley, although the design had been implemented on European machines for some time. Once the Knucklehead was released to the world, motorcycle riding in the USA would never be the same.

◆ In the first year of production, the new Knucklehead motor was offered only in a 61-cubic inch version.
◆ Three EL varieties were sold in a choice of medium compression, high compression or a model with sidecar gearing.
◆ A four-speed transmission was included among the Knucklehead's new hardware array.

Owner: Wheels Through Time Museum

Mounted to the top of the fuel tank was another first for Harley in 1936: an instrument pod holding a large, circular speedometer, gauges and ignition switch. This feature is still a trademark of the Harley-Davidson motorcycles today. The EL was a popular high-compression model for Harley in 1936. A total of 1,526 of the bikes were produced. The EL and E were the only overhead-valve models remaining in the H-D lineup by 1936. All the other bikes featured side-valve motors.

1937 MODEL EL

Harley-Davidsons had been pressed into police duty by the California Highway Patrol since 1925, and this 1937 was just another example of the family bloodline. A slightly altered air cleaner, along with the CHP paint were the only outward changes visible to the official-use-only machine.

◆ Speedometers on the CHP Harleys read up to 120 mph, versus the 100 seen on civilian models.
◆ The contour of the saddle was enhanced by its own suspension, providing the officer with plenty of comfort during his tour.
◆ The chrome case guards were on duty to protect the officer's legs in the event of a crash.

1938 MODEL EL

Having been introduced only two model years earlier, the Knucklehead-powered models from Harley were proving to be a popular choice. Still only sold in 61-inch displacement, the EL outsold the next most popular choice by a margin of 2 to 1.

◆ A fully enclosed valve train was new for the 1938 EL models.
◆ Additional frame augmentation provided a better platform for increasing power levels.
◆ $435 was required to ride home on a new EL in 1938.

Owner: National Motorcycle Museum

1938 MODEL U

The Flathead models continued to fill most of Harley's catalogs in 1938. An ever-increasing list of applications found motorcycles being pressed into a variety of new duties. This Package Delivery machine could carry a sizeable payload in its rectangular housing.

◆ **The U was the medium-compression model in the 74-cid lineup for 1938.**
◆ **The U was also available with a sidecar.**
◆ **The U's side-valve engine was mated to a four-speed transmission.**

Owner: Al & Pat Doerman

1939 MODEL EL

1939 was another year of incremental changes to the line, and even the popular Knucklehead motor was only altered slightly. Internal modifications delivered a mild boost in the horsepower department, as well as providing better shifting. Better springs on the front fork also enhanced comfort and handling.

◆ **The EL motor displaced 61 cubic inches and was the high-compression variant.**
◆ **Although the EL was fitted with a smaller motor than some of the other 1939 models, it outsold them by a wide margin.**
◆ **2,695 ELs were sold at a price of $435 each in 1939.**

Owner: Pierce Harley-Davidson

1939 MODEL EL

The classic contours of the 1939 EL make it one of America's favorites. The balance of shape, color and dimensions add up to what many consider to be the perfect design for a motorcycle.

◆ The EL and ES models for 1939 had improved springs on the front fork.
◆ The EL was the high-compression version of the 61-cid motor for 1939 and sold for $435.
◆ The "cat's-eye" dashboard atop the fuel tank was one of the universal changes on 1939 Harleys.

Owner: National Motorcycle Museum

1940 MODEL EL

The latest year for Harley would introduce a number of incremental changes. All 1940 big-twin models now featured a horizontally ribbed timing case cover on the right side of the motor. New semi-circular floorboards replaced the previous rectangular versions.

◆ **The latest fuel tank badges were teardrop shaped and cast in steel.**
◆ **A larger Linkert carburetor was installed on the 61-cubic inch motors.**
◆ **Sales of the EL outstripped all other Harleys by a substantial margin.**

The Knucklehead motor retained the same 61-cubic inch displacement, but was assembled using a few enhanced components for 1940. Early examples of the OHV mill were built using internal oil baffles, but they were removed from the 1940 motors. A larger venturi made for easier breathing as the 61 gained in power and durability. The EL continued to be by far the most popular Harley in 1940, with 3,893 bikes produced. The EL and ES (the EL with a sidecar) were the only overhead-valve models in the 1940 lineup. Prices for 1940 Harleys ranged from $350 for the 45-cid side-valve Model WL TO $530 for the Model GDT large box Servi-Car.

1941 MODEL FL

1941 would be the first year for the bigger 74-cubic inch V-twin power plant from Harley, and it was a welcome addition. As motorcycles were being pressed into more duties, added power was becoming a daily request from owners. Identical in appearance to the smaller EL and ES motors, the new FL and FS models provided a much-needed boost in horsepower and torque.

◆ Both the FL and FS motors were mated to four-speed transmissions.
◆ 2,452 copies of the newly minted FL were sold in 1941.
◆ The $465 FL entry fee was $40 higher than the 61-cubic inch EL.

Owner: Walters Brothers Harley-Davidson

1941 MODEL WL

The WL was one of 14 side-valve bikes for 1941. The 45-cubic inch motor of the WL shifted through a three-speed transmission, while others used four gears. The simplicity of the WL resulted in the highest sales of the line that year.

◆ **4,277 WLs were sold in 1941, which was nearly double the next model in line.**
◆ **The $350 price tag also helped push the lowly WL to the top of the sales charts.**
◆ **A compression ratio of 4.75:1 was now found on all WL and Servi-Car models.**

Owner: Wheels Through Time Museum

1942 MODEL UL

Very few machines built during WWII were purchased by civilians, and this 1942 UL was originally used by the armed forces. Powered by the 74-cubic inch Flathead motor, it provided adequate power on and off the base.

◆ The UL motor featured high compression and shifted through a four-speed gearbox.
◆ 750 Harleys were being produced each week in June of 1942.
◆ Only 405 examples of the UL were produced for the model year.

By 1942, the Flathead motor had proven its worth, and was being pressed into new levels of service with every passing year of production. The H-D plant produced nearly 22,000 military bikes for 1942, and little attention was given to the UL and other civilian models. The UL was one of 13 models in the Harley lineup to start the year, and one of eight side-valve twins.

1942 MODEL WLA

As was true with every manufacturer in the U.S., H-D production shifted to fulfill wartime needs during WWII. More than 80,000 of the WLAs were shipped overseas and put into active duty. Many saw action on the battlegrounds, while others were pressed into use on military bases.

◆ The WLA was driven by a 45-cubic inch, Flathead motor that shifted through a three-speed gearbox.
◆ The WLA was used by the U.S. military, while the WLC was built for the Canadian Armed Forces.
◆ Durability was tantamount as the WLAs put into duty would see a wide variety of conditions, few of which were pleasant.

Owner: Henry Hardin family

When equipped for use on the battlefield, the WLA came complete with ammo boxes, a Thompson submachine gun, extra ground and fender clearance, and often times the fabric and plastic windscreen. With a government military contract calling for 31,393 motorcycles to be built over two years, Harley stepped up production and built 13,051 WLA models in 1942. The headlight was moved to the front fender to help avoid crash damage. A rectangular oil filter replaced the cylindrical design of earlier models.

1942 MODEL XA

To fulfill another government contract, Harley-Davidson produced 1,000 copies of the XA for military use. Powered by a horizontally opposed, twin-cylinder motor that displaced 45 cubic inches, the XA had a much different profile than the WLA. Ruggedly built with a hydraulic front fork, the XA was ready for any action a soldier could throw at it.

◆ **The installation of larger balloon type tires helped the XA to keep its footing when riding over desert sand.**
◆ **The placement of the cylinders aided in keeping the motor cool in hot climates.**
◆ **This example of the XA has fenders that include a small lip while others were fitted with flat sheet metal versions.**

Owner: Kersting's Harley-Davidson

1946 MODEL E

As with almost every faction of the American manufacturing scene, Harley was still recovering from the war effort in 1946. Very few changes were made to the latest machines as assembly lines ramped up for future sales. The E was fitted by a medium compression, 61-cubic inch motor, and had four gears to choose from.

◆ Replacing the wartime horsehair saddle filler with "spun" latex foam returned some comfort to the civilian rider.
◆ Steering head geometry was changed to 30 degrees, but did nothing to improve handling.
◆ Sticker price on the 1946 E was $463.67.

Owner: Les White

1947 MODEL FL SPORT SOLO

1947 was the final year of the Knucklehead motor from Harley-Davidson. The FL Sport Solo was considered to be the finest model offered that year, and it provided the buyer with a wide range of features. This example has been fitted with leather saddlebags, chrome luggage rack and case guards.

◆ The "FL" designated that the machine had a high compression, 74-cubic inch motor.
◆ Harley produced 6,900 copies to meet with growing demand, making the FL Sport Solo by far the most popular model for 1947.
◆ Carrying a retail price of $605, the big FL seemed like a true luxury purchase.

Owner: Pierce Harley-Davidson

1947 SERVI-CAR

First sold in 1933, the Servi-Car remained in the sales catalog and was often utilized by law enforcement agencies. The stable three-wheel platform proved to be a vital addition to motor pools. Typically used in parade or parking enforcement capacities, the Servi-Car would stay in the lineup for many years to come.

◆ **The Servi-Car had a 40-year model run that ended in 1973.**
◆ **Many Servi-Cars were purchased with tow bars to be used by automotive service departments.**
◆ **A 45-cubic inch side-valve motor was used in every year of the Servi-Car's life.**

Owner: Harley-Davidson Archives

1948 MODEL FL

1948 marked the first year of sale for the all-new Panhead-powered Harleys. The new motor was a vast improvement over the previous Knucklehead due in part to its better cooling. Sold in either 61- or 74-cubic inch versions, the newest models from Harley represented a significant step in H-D history.

◆ Aluminum-alloy cylinder heads were mounted to the V-twin motor, providing better cooling.
◆ The new hydraulic valve train ran quieter and required less maintenance than the old Knucklehead.
◆ Horsepower for the new EL motor was unchanged. The mill was rated at 40 hp @ 4800 rpm.

Owner: Wheels Through Time Museum

The FL was the high-compression 74-cubic inch bike in Harley's 1948 lineup. One notable change was that the speedometer face was modified for 1948. The large, circular face was now blue with white numerals that read 10 through 120. More than 8,000 FL bikes were produced for 1948 at a cost of $650 each. The FL was one of three overhead-valve twin models in the 1948 lineup, with each engine displacing 74 cid. The frame was slightly modified in 1948 and allowed more room for the taller engine.

1948 MODEL WL

The trio of Flathead-powered Harleys was diminished to a single variant in 1948 as the 74- and 80-cubic inch models faded from view. The WL continued on, powered by the 45-cubic inch side-valve power plant.

◆ The 45-cubic inch motor would be replaced in 1952 by the new K models, except for the Servi-Car.
◆ A three-speed transmission was still used to select the required gear.
◆ Production of the 1948 WL only totaled 2,124 units, even though it was the lowest-priced V-twin in the catalog.

Owner: Dave Monahan

1948 MODEL WR

Flat track racing remained one of the most popular forms of competitive motorsports, and the WR claimed a huge number of victories. Based on the civilian WL, the WR received a full complement of upgrades and performance enhancements.

◆ Devoid of any lighting or excess sheet metal, the WR was race ready.
◆ The 45-cubic inch side-valve motor proved both reliable and powerful.
◆ Many private racing efforts involved riding the WR to the track, racing all day, then riding home again.

Owner: Mike Millay

STAR NEWS NEWSPAPERS
STAR NEWS
NEWSPAPERS
MORNING EVENING
SUNDAY

1949 MODEL FLP

The powerful big-twin models from Milwaukee had proven their ability to deliver the rider and a payload with aplomb. By adding a package delivery box to the machine, capacity grew by leaps and bounds. A wide variety of businesses now put the durable Panhead-powered machines into daily duty.

◆ The Panhead motor was introduced in the 1948 models, and grew in popularity with every passing week.

◆ The F models displaced 74 cubic inches, while the E motor remained at 61.

◆ The FL featured a high-compression motor and a four-speed transmission.

Owner: American Classic Motorcycle Co.

1949 MODEL FL

Following the introduction of the Panhead motor in 1948, Harley-Davidson added a hydraulic front fork and the Hydra-Glide was born. In 1949, the buyer could opt for the new forks, or get the older springer version. This would be the final year for the springer option as the Hydra-Glide proved to be extremely popular.

◆ The new front forks were comprised of internal springs with hydraulic damping.
◆ The 1949 Hydra-Glides had the lower section of their fork legs painted black.
◆ More than 8,000 copies of the new FL were assembled in 1949, easily eclipsing all other models sold by Harley that year.

Owner: Kersting's Harley-Davidson

1950 MODEL FL

First introduced in 1948, the Panhead motors from Harley were a big step forward in cooling and performance. For 1950, both the E and F series motors gained an extra 10 percent in horsepower as a result of their reconfigured heads. The lower section of the fork legs were also finished in their original steel versus the earlier painted variety.

♦ **Six different models were driven by the improved Panhead motor for 1950.**

♦ **The most popular choice was the FL, which accounted for 7,407 sales that year.**

♦ **The F, FL and FS models each sold for $750 a copy.**

Owner: Mike Butala

1952 MODEL FL

The big 74-cubic inch FL remained the popular choice amongst buyers, and minor changes to the 1952s improved the breed. Valves were "Parko-Lubricized" to enhance operation and longevity, and rotating exhaust valves were applied late in the production run.

◆ A new hand-clutch, foot-shift option was first seen on the 1952 FL.
◆ Methods of mounting of the motor and toolbox were also improved in 1952.
◆ 1952 would mark the final year of sale for the smaller 61-cubic inch Panhead models.

Owner: John Archaki

Popularity of the bigger 74-cubic inch Panhead motor would bring about the demise of the smaller 61-cubic inch motor at the end of production in 1952. All the F models could be had in two-tone color schemes for 1952. The FL model retained the hand shift, while the FLF had the foot shift. The FL sold for $1,025 in 1954. A total of 4,757 of these models rolled out of the factory.

1952 MODEL K

The K Model was new for 1952. With a 45-cubic inch motor nestled in its frame, it was not the most powerful Harley sold, but it bristled with new technology. Cylinder heads and pistons were all formed from an aluminum alloy, and a side-valve configuration was applied. The hand-clutch, foot-shift arrangement was a bit out of the ordinary, but would become the accepted method of choosing gears.

◆ K Models featured Harley's first use of hydraulic suspension at both ends of the chassis.

◆ The four-speed gearbox was now an integral part of the engine case, another first for H-D.

◆ A 4.5-gallon fuel tank was aboard to provide the rider with more miles between gas station stops.

Owner: National Motorcycle Museum

1954 MODEL KH

First introduced in 1952, the K models continued to be a popular alternative for buyers. The KH took over for the now-extinct K model in 1954, bringing new improvements to the fray. A redesigned gearbox/crankcase brought a new level of rigidity to the game, and internal motor mods added some punch.

◆ **A bolstered frame helped keep the more powerful KH under control.**
◆ **The 55-cubic inch KH motor delivered 12 percent more horsepower than the previous edition.**
◆ **With a retail cost of $925, 1,579 KH units were produced for the 1954 model year.**

1954 MODEL FL POLICE

The flexibility offered by two-wheeled patrol bikes continued to be the driving factor in their use in police departments. Whether put into active patrol duty, or simply used as parade vehicles, the Big Twins from Milwaukee were welcomed by law enforcement and civilians alike.

◆ Even police-equipped Harleys came complete with the 50th anniversary badge on the front fenders.
◆ The radio gear was stashed in one of the steel saddlebags, leaving the other open for ticket books and patrol materials.
◆ The large fabric windscreen added some versatility and comfort for officers on highway patrols.

Owner: American Classic Motorcycle Co.

1954 MODEL FL

1954 models were festooned with golden front fender badges to commemorate the 50th year of production for Harley-Davidson. This example is also fitted with grips and kick-start pedal molded in the same "Anniversary" yellow as the machine.

◆ **Three different frame configurations were employed during the production run of 1954 Big Twin models.**

◆ **The new Jubilee horn replaced the previous circular warning device, and became an instant classic.**

◆ **The FL was the most popoular model in 1954, racking up 4,757 sales.**

Owner: John Archaki

1955 MODEL FL

The FLF designation was in reference to the latest style of selecting gears. Early versions of almost all motorcycles utilized a foot-clutch and hand-shift operation. The first of the foot-shift models from Harley appeared in 1952, and were becoming the first choice for many riders.

◆ A revised mounting system for the intake manifold made accessing the carburetor an easier task on the 1955s.

◆ A change to rubber-impregnated asbestos base gaskets was also made.

◆ Of the twin-cylinder models built in 1955, the FLF was tops in production.

Owner: John Parham

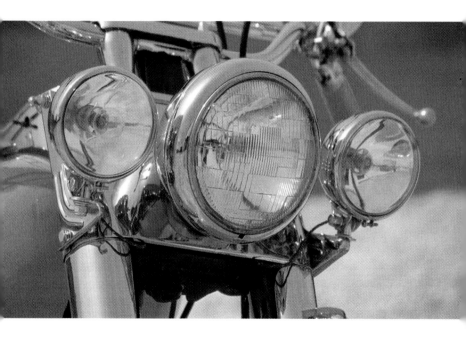

Adding a pair of accessory driving lamps was a common practice on the big FL models. The fabulous FLF was the low-compression "Big Twin" offering from Harley in 1955.

A revised tank badge was used for the first time on the 1955 models, helping to distinguish them from other production years. The FLF was one of six different F models in the H-D lineup for 1955. The models shared the same 74-cubic inch engine, but differed in compression, shifting and other smaller details. The popular FLF was a 74-cid model with a four-speed transmission and no reverse gear.

1956

1956 MODEL FL

Big Twins for 1956 received a few minor alterations, but the swoopy graphics were all new. The speedometers also changed again, receiving new luminescent numerals and a brighter, red indicator needle. 1956 would be the final appearance for the FLE and FLEF "Traffic" models.

♦ **High compression FLH models wore colorful decals on the oil bag stating the designation.**
♦ **The 1956 FL models continued to have hand shifting.**
♦ **A new air cleaner and cover were installed to help breathing and filtration.**

Owner: Harley-Davidson Archives

1956 MODEL KH

This 1956 KH was altered like all the rest, but has the definite distinction of having been owned by none other than Elvis Presley himself. 1956 would be the final year for the KH and KHK models.

♦ A modified frame and altered shocks at the rear provided a lower saddle height.
♦ A new taillight housing was stamped in steel, then painted to match the chosen color of the bike.
♦ Only 539 KH models were built in 1956, making them scarce today.

Owner: Harley-Davidson Archives

1956 MODEL KHK

Alongside the more timid KH, the KHK delivered a higher level of performance in a similar machine. The KHK was the recipient of more aggressive cams, lower bars and less chrome than the KH.

◆ 1956 would be the last time the KH and KHK were sold. The all-new XL arrived in 1957.
◆ With the exception of the Servi-Car, the KH and KHK were the final machines built by Harley with Flathead motors.
◆ 714 KHKs were built in 1956. They sold for $1,003 apiece.

1957 MODEL XL

Replacing the K models, the all new XL arrived for the 1957 model year. The XL was not a homologation of older machines, but built using fresh designs and hardware. The 55-cubic inch motor featured overhead valves, just like the XL's bigger FL brethren.

◆ **Aluminum pistons rode within the cast-iron cylinders, and hemispherical heads topped off the jugs.**
◆ **The speedometer was housed in the same enclosure that finished off the telescopic forks.**
◆ **Carrying a retail price of $1,103, the XL sold very well in its first year and nearly 2,000 bikes rolled out of the factory.**

Owner: Pierce Harley-Davidson

The brand new Sportster was designed and built with a variety of fresh concepts, including the "Sportster" name cast into the side cover of the 55-cubic inch motor. The model was Harley's response to the growing number of British sport bikes on U.S. roads.

◆ The new Sportster used a previously designed crank case, but with new heads grafted on.

◆ The guts of the XL engine included aluminum pistons and hemispheric combustion chambers.

◆ The four-speed transmission was shifted by foot, with a lever mounted on the right side of the bike.

1957 MODEL FLHF

The best seller in the 1957 family was the FLHF. The big 74-cubic inch mill offered the rider the choice of four gears which were selected using the foot-shift control. This example has been outfitted with every accessory sold in the day. From the two-tone windscreen to the fringed saddle and bags, not an inch of this great machine had been overlooked.

◆ **The introduction of the XL kept changes to the FL models at a minimum.**
◆ **Steel alloy guides were added to both intake and exhaust valves.**
◆ **Valve springs were also enhanced in the middle of the production period.**

Owner: John Archaki

As was typical, the paint arrangements for the latest year were different than the year before. The latest tank badge was to be a 1957 only design. The FLHF remained a flagship of the H-D lineup, with a classic design and proven track record on the sales front.

1958 MODEL FL

1949 had witnessed the advent of a hydraulic front fork being added to the big FL models, and 1958 would take the next logical step. By adding rear suspension to the big-twins, the Duo-Glide line was created. A new system of supporting the rear fender was also implemented to meet with the changing rear ends.

◆ The newly suspended rear end also received a hydraulic drum brake in 1958.

◆ A single exhaust pipe was on hand to expel spent gases.

◆ The latest frame configuration resulted in changes to the oil filter mounting, and the oil-return line was enhanced.

Owner: Paul Ross

1958 MODEL XLCH

To feed the hunger for high-performance bikes, the XLCH was introduced in 1958. The XLCH was stripped of all amenities, like lighting and a battery, in an effort to save weight and boost performance. The short exhaust pipes did little to muffle sound, but also bumped up the power delivery.

◆ "Bobbed" fenders both front and rear harkened back to early days of "run what you brung" events at local tracks.
◆ Magneto ignitions were in charge of providing energy to the spark plugs.
◆ Although the XLCH was designed for sport riding, there was suspension at both ends.

Owner: Don Chasteen

1959 MODEL FLF

The accessory catalog was growing with each new model year, and many owners had trouble resisting temptation to buy every option offered. This example has been fitted with the backrest, saddlebags, driving lights and extra chrome.

◆ The foot-shift FL model was becoming a more popular choice, but the high-compression FLHF was still the sales leader in 1959.

◆ Every 1959 "Big Twin" was motivated by the 74-cubic inch mill.

◆ With 1,222 FLFs built in 1959, the model ranked third on the production chart.

Owner: American Classic Motorcycle Co.

1959 MODEL FLF

The Panhead-powered machines were being utilized in a wide variety of duties. This 1959 was used as a funeral escort.

◆ **The FL models received only minor tweaks in 1959, including neutral indicator lights on the FLF and FLHF, and slightly different fender trim.**
◆ **The FL lineup included high- and low-compression versions, and hand- and foot-shift models. The FLF had the foot shift.**

Owner: Al & Pat Doerman

1959 MODEL XLCH

For some Harley buyers, performance won out over comfort, and for them the XLCH was the only answer. Driven by a high-compression 55-cubic inch motor, the lighter weight XLCH proved its worth at many motorsports venues.

◆ **The XLCH was first seen in 1958, and was not street legal in its first year of sale.**
◆ **By adding an electrical system, head and taillights, as well as a horn, the XLCH was made street ready.**
◆ **The 1959 XLCH was the only Harley that year not to receive the latest "Arrow-Flite" tank logo.**

1959 MODEL FLHF

The FLHF was the top dog in both production and equipment for 1960. The high-compression, 74-cubic inch motor was shifted with a hand clutch and foot shift. Tank graphics were once again changed for the latest model year.

◆ Carrying a price tag of $1,375, the FLHF was third in the price sheets in 1960.
◆ Only minor revisions were made to the FL family in 1960.
◆ Both the headlight nacelle and handlebars had a two-piece construction for 1960.

Owner: John Archaki

The dual-exhaust still featured the crossover design that set the big FL models apart from the crowd. Harley-Davidson produced almost 6,000 of its Duo-Glide models for 1960. This lineup included the FLHF. Though H-D unveiled its new 165cc Topper model in 1960, and the Sportster series was still a big part of the lineup, the big overhead-valve twin F models were still the anchors of the H-D menu.

1961 MODEL FLF

1961 was another year of only incremental changes across the board for Harley-Davidson. The FLF was the 74-cubic inch, low-compression model that shifted with a foot control. A four-speed gearbox was still in place.

◆ Fully equipped with two-tone windscreen, trimmed saddle and leather saddlebags, this FLF was ready for anything.

◆ Additional bits of chrome also helped to set this example apart from the crowd.

◆ $1,335 was required to ride a new FLF home in 1961—a $25 increase from the 1960 model.

Owner: "Mac" McHugh

Every 1961 model except the Topper was decorated with the latest in tank art, including this FLF model The latest graphics package was joined by newly cast badges as well. The FLF carried a sticker price of $1,335—the same price as its hand-shifting sibling, the FL. With less than 5,000 "Big Twins" rolling off the assembly lines, production of Harley's signature big bikes was down in 1961 in the face of increasing Japanese competition.

The Jubilee trumpet horn remained a popular item on the big FL models, and the use of chrome case guards was becoming more common.

1963 MODEL FLF

Changes to the 1963 FL line were again minor, but made the Big Twin models a better breed. A wider rear drum brake, complete with an enhanced hydraulic cylinder, made stopping an easier task. A larger chain guard allowed for easier servicing of the improved brake layout. Another change to the tank graphics was joined by revised tank badges.

♦ Of the four FL models produced in 1963, the FLF ended up in third place on the sales charts.
♦ Another $25 bump in MSRP brought the FLF to $1,360 for 1963.
♦ Turn signals at both ends were modified and relocated.

Owner: Greg Lew

1963 MODEL AH TOPPER

The Topper models were carry-overs from the previous year, and the low-compression AU model production did not reach double-digits in 1963. The addition of the sidecar provided some utility to the diminutive machines, but did nothing to boost power.

◆ The Topper was unchanged except for a new logo.
◆ The Topper lasted one more year, through 1964, before it disappeared. Less than 1,000 were produced for 1963.
◆ The Topper was available with an optional sidecar.

1964 MODEL FLHF

With the introduction of the next generation Big Twin models pending, 1964 was a quiet year of changes for Harley-Davidson. Besides the revised tank graphics, the FLHF was the recipient of a new two-key system and a wider Jiffy stand. Late 1964 models also got two-piece chain guards.

◆ Total production for the FLH and FLHF for 1964 was 2,725.

◆ An improved oil pressure switch was also implemented on the '64 FL models.

◆ Prices for the FLHF increased to $1,450 for the latest model year.

1964 MODEL XLCH

Another model that was largely unchanged between 1963 and '64 was the XLCH. A wider front brake was installed on the XLH and XLCH to improve stopping power. The lower fork bracket was now finished in chrome versus the black version seen in 1963.

◆ The XLCH was still the performance choice for many riders.

◆ The fuel tanks now wore white side panels to contrast with the chosen color.

◆ The selling price of $1,360 put the XLCH within $90 of the bigger FLH models.

Owner: Larry Andersen

1965 MODEL FLFB-A

The addition of the electric start was a big new addition for 1965. The big FL twins were now brought to life with the touch of a button. The kick-start pedals were still in place in the event of an unplanned battery loss. The ElectraGlide delivered Harley-Davidson into the new era of riding convenience.

- ◆ **A larger 12-volt system was implanted to power up the new starter.**
- ◆ **The previous "horseshoe" oil tank was supplanted with a rectangular version to make room for the bigger battery.**
- ◆ **Hand-shift models were still offered, but were losing popularity.**

1965 MODEL FLFB

For those riders who demanded a truly custom machine, Harley continued to offer a wide variety of accessories and add-ons. The two-person "Buddy" seat has been teamed with a pair of white leather saddlebags on this FLFB. A chrome front fender rail and windscreen offer flash and protection.

◆ The foot-shifting models in the FL line got new 5-gallon gas tanks to replace the old 3.7-gallon models. The hand-shift bikes kept the smaller tanks for another year.

◆ The kick start wasn't needed, but it still remained on the FL models.

◆ The "B" designation was applied to all models that had the electric start.

Owner: Illinois Harley-Davidson

The newly inaugurated ElectraGlide models wore the new nameplate on the front fender, replacing the previous Duo-Glide badges.

1965 MODEL S-165 HUMMER

The S-165 was little more than an enlarged version of the earlier S-125, first seen in 1947. The Italian powered models never reached as many buyers as Harley had envisioned, but they did bring many first-time riders into the Harley-Davidson showrooms.

◆ The S-165 was also referred to as the M-165.
◆ In 1953, the S-165 was bumped to the larger 165cc displacement from the previous 125cc variety.
◆ To satisfy buyers of the earlier 125cc version, the 125 Hummer returned to the catalog in 1954 and was sold until 1959.

1966 MODEL C SPRINT

With hopes of making up some ground on the onslaught of Japanese imports, Harley began selling the Italian built Sprints in 1962. Powered by a 250cc, single-cylinder motor, they aimed these machines at the rider who was intimidated by the full-size models from Milwaukee.

◆ Aermacchi was the manufacturer of the motors, but most of the remaining components were brought in from other suppliers.

◆ The original 250cc motors were enlarged to 350cc in 1969 to deliver added power.

◆ 1974 was the final year of sale for the four-stroke Sprints as a few two-stroke entries were added to the mix.

Owner: Paul Ross

1966 MODEL FLHFB

Big news for the 1966 lineup was the introduction of the latest Shovelhead motors. The new "Power Pac" aluminum heads were bolted to the earlier jugs, creating the newest iteration of the Big Twin motor. Cooler operating temperatures and a 10-percent boost in horsepower were two big selling points for the 1966 FL models.

◆ The latest head design also resulted in a drastic reduction in oil leaks.
◆ The first Shovelhead motors were mated to a die-cast zinc carburetor from Linkert.
◆ 1974 was the final year of sale for the four-stroke Sprints as a few two-stoke entries were added to the mix.

Owner: Illinois Harley-Davidson

1967 MODEL FLFB

With the introduction of the ElectraGlides in 1966, 1967 was a slow year for changes. New Tillotson carburetors were installed on the latest FLB models, but the results were not positive. The problems were not enough to keep them off the Big Twins until 1970. Revised tank graphics were used along with the same badges as before.

◆ Sealed, ball-bearing wheel hubs were introduced on the FLBs.
◆ A modified rear brake drum resulted in changes to the axle and spacer.
◆ New on the options list were the latest "turnout" exhaust pipes.

Owner: American Classic Motorcycle Co.

1967 MODEL XLH

The XLH was fitted with an electric starter for 1967, putting it on the same playing field as the bigger FLB models. A newly shaped side case provided the required space for the starter mechanism used on the XLH. The XLCH also received the new cover, but retained the kick-start hardware.

◆ 2,000 copies of the XLH and XLCH were produced in 1967.

◆ The $1,600 asking price of the XLCH was within $200 of the bigger FLHB and FLHFB models.

◆ Rear suspension on the XL models was also reworked on the 1967 units.

Owner: Al & Pat Doerman

1968 MODEL XLCH

Changes on 1968 XLCH were nominal as the model seemed to sell fairly well as it was. Improved front fork damping and another inch of travel made up the alterations for the newest versions being sold.

◆ The peanut tank held little more than 2 gallons of fossil fuel.

◆ A retail cost of $1,600 was attached to every XLCH built that year.

◆ Production of the XLCH handily beat the XLH, with a tally of 4,900 to 1,975 for the XLH.

Owner: Ted Moran

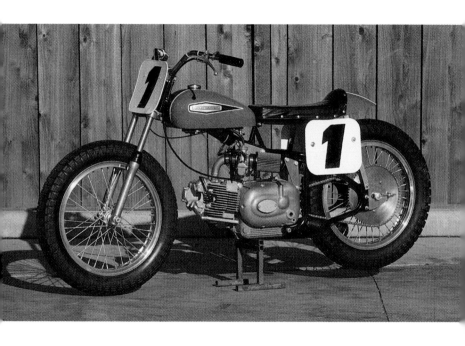

1968 MODEL CR250

With its heritage based on the Italian-built Aermacchi models, the CR250 was a purpose-built race machine. Devoid of excess sheet metal, lights or non-essential racing gear, the CR tipped the scales at just over 200 lbs. The 250cc motor provided plenty of energy to move the small machine along with ease.

◆ As delivered, the CR ran with increased compression and a low-restriction exhaust.
◆ The frame was built without rear suspension and the front fork only delivered the minimum required for racing.
◆ The CR250 dominated at flat track events all across the country.

Owner: Dave Kiesow

1969 MODEL SS

In an effort to boost sales of the Sprint models, both the on- and off-road versions were gifted with an extra 100ccs of displacement. The street going version seen here was now known as the SS, while the off-road variant would become the ERS. The new 350cc motors still stirred four-speed gearboxes, and sales remained flat.

◆ The single-cylinder power plants were from Aermacchi, an Italian builder.
◆ 4,575 copies of the SS were built for 1969, while only 250 of the ERS were required.
◆ Harley's smaller-displacement bikes faced a big challenge from the latest Japanese entries.

Owner: Harley-Davidson Archives

1970 MODEL XLH

Ignition systems on the XLH and XLCH were improved on the 1970 models. Earlier versions received the spark from a generator, but that was replaced by a coil and points. A "boat tail" rear fender unit could also be ordered on the new XLH, but its reception was less than enthusiastic.

◆ Being used as a more luxurious ride, this XLH has been upgraded with saddlebags and passenger backrest.
◆ The windscreen and leather storage case were more comfort options.
◆ Only 3,033 copies of the XLH were built, while 5,527 of the XLCH were produced for the 1970 model year.

Owner: Don Chasteen

1971 MODEL XLH

A controversial option on two of the 1971 Harleys was the "boat tail" rear fender. Formed from fiberglass, the optional hardware was certainly not traditional. The XLH was still powered by the same 55-cubic inch motor as the XLCH, and both shifted through four-speed transmissions.

◆ All 1971 Sportsters were fitted with wet clutches in place of the previous dry-plate variety.
◆ Fewer than 4,000 copies of the XLH were sold this year, and only a handful were purchased with the ungainly rear fender option.
◆ Sparkling Turquoise and Sparkling America were two color options for 1971.

Owner: Pierce Harley-Davidson

1971 MODEL FX

An all-new model, the FX was first introduced for the 1971 model year. By blending the frame of the FL with the front forks of the XL, the FX was born. The tanks could carry 3.5 gallons of fuel, and an instrument panel was mounted to the top, just like the big FL models.

◆ The 74-cubic inch Shovelhead motor was used to power the new FX.

◆ The new configuration weighed 70 lbs. less than the FL, but the XL forks proved to be troublesome on the bigger chassis.

◆ 4,700 copies of the FX were produced in its first year.

Owner: Harley-Davidson Archives

The "boat tail" rear fender was first seen on the 1970 XLH models, and even then the response was decidedly mixed. It seemed to earn a love/hate opinion from the cycle buying market, and 1971 would be the only year it was used on the FX. The FX had a 16-inch rear wheel and 19-inch front wheel. The FX was also a kick-start-only model.

1971 MODEL 71MSR BAJA

The Baja returned for a second year of sale in 1971, and filled the needs of a few buyers that required their small off-road machine to be Harley-built. The 100cc motor remained a bundle of performance hardware in a small package. A variety of tweaks to the single-cylinder mill delivered 12 horsepower—enough to create an entertaining and useful machine.

◆ The Baja was also known as the 71MSR in the catalogs.
◆ A five-speed gearbox was used, and a choice of close or wide ratios could be had.
◆ A compression ratio of 11.5:1, along with ported cylinders, helped to bump the output of the tiny motor.

Owner: Harley-Davidson Archives

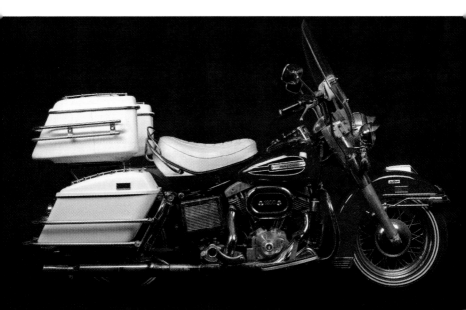

1972 MODEL FLH

After the AMF merger, production of Harley-Davidson was growing, but the quantity of factory defects was keeping pace. Efforts were being made to produce better machines, but it would take time for the results to become obvious. Changes to the 1972 FL consisted of the addition of a front disc brake. With the drum on the rear wheel, bringing the 700-lb. behemoth to rest was an easier chore now.

◆ Accessories were being added at a rapid pace, as seen here in the Tour Pak and saddlebags.
◆ The smaller XL models were being produced about twice as fast as the big FL models in 1972.
◆ Plastic switch housings were first seen on the 1972 models in an attempt to save weight.

Owner: American Classic Motorcycle Co.

1972 MODEL MC SHORTSTER

New for 1972 was the dwarf-like Shortster. Powered by a 65cc Aermacchi single-cylinder motor, it was hardly a rocket. Intended for younger, first-time riders, it would see many adult miles as a pit bike, or for running around at large events.

◆ A three-speed gearbox offered plenty of flexibility to whoever was aboard.
◆ 8,000 units were assembled for the Shortster, also known as Model MC, during its first year.
◆ The two-stroke motor delivered decent power to the tiny rear wheel.

Owner: Harley-Davidson Archives

1973 MODEL FL ELECTRAGLIDE

Buyers of the 1973 FL models would find a variety of upgrades to their beloved ElectraGlide. A second disc brake was mounted to the rear wheel. Now each wheel had its own disc, and the combination slowed the big FL much more effectively. Since the bike had been converted to electric start in 1966, the kick start hardware was obsolete, and finally removed from the 1973 units.

- ◆ **The hand shift option was no longer offered in 1973.**
- ◆ **Contours of the taillight lens were revised for the latest model year.**
- ◆ **Only 1,025 FLs were built for 1973, while 7,750 FLH models were assembled.**

The FL models were being ridden for longer distances as their mechanics improved. The application of saddlebags, two-person Buddy seat and rear luggage rack added to the utility and convenience.

1975 MODEL XR750

Introduced in 1969, the XR750 was an overnight success. Riders took the XR to numerous dirt track victories at racing venues all across the country. Early examples ran with iron cylinder heads, but they were later fitted with heads cast in aluminum.

◆ The V-twin motor from the XL was used as the base to build the XR mill.
◆ A pair of Mikuni carburetors could be opened fully with only a quarter turn of the throttle.
◆ The performance enhancements delivered 90 horsepower to the rider's hand.

Owner: Wheels Through Time Museum

1975 MODEL SS-250

In its ongoing efforts to entice new riders to the flock, Harley offered a long line of smaller machines in 1960s and '70s. The SS-250 was new for 1975, and was basically an enlarged version of the previous 175 variants. The "SS" moniker told the buyer the machine was built for the street, and the "250" referred to the displacement of 250 cubic centimeters.

◆ The single cylinder motor was a two-stroke, and shifted through a five-speed gearbox.
◆ While the SS-250 was designed for street use, an SX-250 was built for on- and off-road use.
◆ 3,000 units were sold in 1975, putting it in the middle of Harley's sales range for the year.

Owner: Bob McClean

1977 MODEL MX250

Built to enter the newly AMA-sanctioned motocross arena, the MX250 turned out to be fairly competent. Horsepower came compliments of the 250cc Aermacchi motor, using a two-stroke design and a single cylinder.

◆ The chrome-moly chassis featured front forks direct from Japan.
◆ Rear shocks were of the latest remote-reservoir variety and helped keep the rear wheel planted.
◆ Despite the performance it delivered, the MX250 was only around for 1977 and 1978.

Owner: Dave Kiesow

1977 MODEL XLCR

With entries from Japan flooding into the U.S., Harley needed a machine to compete with the sportier hardware. The XLCR was intended to fill the gap in the Milwaukee -built catalog. The blacked-out entry featured many exclusive bits, but the overall result never caught on with Harley buyers.

◆ The flat-black, Siamese exhaust pipes were one of the more exotic components found on the XLCR.
◆ The "bikini" fairing did not offer much protection from the wind, but added a touch of Euro-bike to the new model.
◆ The fuel tank, rear fender and saddle were also pieces not found on any other Harley.

Owner: National M/C Museum

Among the most distinctive features of the XLCR were the flat black, Siamese exhaust pipes. When teamed up with the rest of the blackened components, the result was simply classic, yet radical for the day.

◆ The XLCR mated the 61-cubic inch overhead-valve twin with a four-speed transmission.
◆ The XLCR was only around for two model years and has become prized by collectors.
◆ The new bike shared its wheels and forks with the FXS of the same year.

1978 MODEL FLHS

With a look that was designed to be reminiscent of the earlier years, the FLHS was a stripped-down variant of the better-dressed machines Harley produced. While the 80-cubic inch motor was soon to be the popular choice, the FLHS was driven by the less-powerful 74-cubic inch V-twin mill.

◆ The double whitewall tires were original equipment on this model.
◆ The chrome battery cover and air cleaner were also part of the standard equipment list.
◆ The "1200" badge on the front fender advertised the smaller-capacity power plant.

Owner: Harley-Davidson Archives

1978 MODEL XLH

To mark its 75th birthday, Harley-Davidson offered a few of its models in special paint and trim. The XLH was the smaller birthday model, but sported several one-year-only details. Black paint was accented by gold pin striping, and the saddle was covered with leather. Gold-colored cast wheels were also on hand to celebrate.

◆ Electronic ignition was added to all XL models for 1978.

◆ Dual disc brakes were mounted to the front wheel and brought the XLH to a safe stop.

◆ 2,323 copies of the XLH Anniversary model were produced for sale.

Owner: Wheels Through Time Museum

1978 MODEL FXS

The Low Riders were first sold for the 1977 model year, and returned for another round in 1978. Their low pillion height and styling were producing strong sales at the dealers. All FXS models were also sparked with electronic ignition. Your choice of all silver or black with silver side panels on the fuel tank were on the option sheet.

◆ A total of 3,742 of these bikes were built for 1977, but that total grew to more than 9,700 for 1978.

◆ By 1979, the FXS was by far the most popular new Harley in the lineup.

◆ The FX, FXE and FXS models changed little for 1978, but the FXS did have a sharp optional silver-and-black paint scheme that set it apart.

1980 MODEL FXWG

1980 was the first year for the "factory custom" FXWG, and it set new standards in the class. With the front fork legs extended by 2 inches, and splayed wider than ever before, the look of the front end was all new. The 21-inch front tire and spoked wheel also set a new direction for Harley.

◆ The Wide Glide style and name was born in 1980, but continues to this day.

◆ The 80-cubic inch Shovelhead motor was mated to a four-speed gearbox.

◆ With the exception of the XLH, the FXWG outsold all other Harley models in 1980.

Owner: Harley-Davidson Archives

The FXWG was an all-new model for 1980 and was designed to look more like a "custom" bike than most factory-built motorcycles. The FXWG featured blacked-out lower engine cases to enhance the black and orange motif. The bi-level saddle was complete with a padded backrest for the passenger.

With the bike being touted as a factory "custom," it would have been foolish to leave off the flame paint job on the FXWG. Nestled within the curves of the applied fire was the official bar and shield of the Motor Company. The FXWG sold well in its first year, with 6,085 bikes rolling out the factory doors.

1980 MODEL FLT

Riding on an all-new chassis, the FLT Tour Glide was more than a new face. An entirely new method of isolating the motor assisted in smoothness and vibration. In addition to the new frame and motor mounts, the FLT came equipped with the latest in fairing designs.

◆ **The hard saddlebags and rear-mounted storage box gave the FLT plenty of capacity for longer journeys.**
◆ **Synthetic, compressible motor mounts made long days in the saddle more appealing with this bike.**
◆ **The drive chain was entirely enclosed, and under constant lubrication.**

Owner: Harley-Davidson Archives

1981 MODEL FLT

Returning for another year, the FLT was mostly unchanged from its debut. The exhaust system was altered to provide better breathing, and a Classic Edition was sold bearing individual paint and graphics.

◆ With 1,636 copies produced for 1981, the FLT was hardly H-D's biggest seller, but it was certainly one of the company's best bikes.

◆ The FLT Tour Guide model was joined by its sibling, the FLTC Tour Glide Classic, that had special paint and graphics.

◆ The FLT bikes had five-speed transmissions, while their 80-cid FLH brethren had four-speed gearboxes.

1982 MODEL FXB STURGIS

The FXB Sturgis edition was first sold as a 1980 model. From its inception it had a drive belt in place of the final chain drive. Having a belt in the transfer case resulted in the double belt designation. The overall black paint was nicely offset with red highlights. A few bits of chrome completed the ensemble.

◆ Very few changes were made to the final edition of the FXB Sturgis for 1982.

◆ Another Sturgis edition would be seen for the 1991 model year.

◆ A set of higher handlebars were fitted with plastic housings for the switches.

Owner: Wheels Through Time Museum

1984 MODEL FXRT

The FXRT model designation was first used in 1983, but the 1984 model had the latest Evolution motor cradled in its frame. The Evolution motor was the next generation of the venerable V-twin power plant from Harley, and incorporated many changes that improved the operation. The new "Blockhead" mill enhanced performance and durability.

◆ **The FXRT was designed for touring, and the frame-mounted fairing provided plenty of protection.**
◆ **The hard saddlebags were capable of stowing enough gear for a long weekend.**
◆ **The new motor proved to be far more reliable than the previous entrant and helped Harley fight off the competition from overseas.**

Owner: Harley-Davidson Archives

The latest version of Harley's 45-degree V-twin motor would be its finest. Improved materials and altered mechanicals would deliver strong drive with fewer leaks than ever before on bikes like the FXRT. This was one of eight models in the FXR family for 1984. The FXRT was named the Sport Glide model.

1984 MODEL XR-1000

Released as a 1983 model first, the XR-1000 was back for another round in 1984. Alloy heads were mated to the existing XL lower end to deliver a potent combination. Dell 'Orto carburetors fed the motor, while a pair of satin black pipes let the spent mixture exit.

◆ The 1984 XR was sold in all silver, or with a black-and-orange color scheme.
◆ Improved brakes allowed the rider better stopping power than before.
◆ 759 of the 1984 XR-1000s were produced, making them relatively scarce today.

Owner: Dave Kiesow

Regardless of what angle you see the XR-1000 from, the look is both distinctive and aggressive. The high-mounted dual exhaust was a trademark of the XR-1000 and added to its racey looks. Sadly, very few buyers took advantage of its single-minded purpose. Despite its limited production numbers, the XR 1000 is considered by many to be one of Harley's finest motorcycles.

1986 MODEL XLH-1100 SPORTSTER

1986 was the first time the Sportster line was fitted with the latest Evolution motors. The XLH-883 and XLH-1100 were not only new names, but bristled with new hardware. The 1100 version wore a plusher saddle, higher bars and a variety of trim pieces not used on the 883 version.

◆ There was almost a $1,200 difference in cost between the two XLH models.

◆ The majority of the motor's cases were new for 1984, and would not fit earlier versions of the Sportster motors.

◆ The higher cost of entry kept production of the XLH-1100 to 3,077 copies.

Owner: Harley-Davidson Archives

The latest iteration of the long-standing Sportster line was the most refined ever. The bigger 1100cc motor also added some needed punch to the often-disrespected model.

1988 MODEL FXSTS SPRINGER SOFTAIL

Introduced the same year as The Motor Company's 85th birthday, the new Springer Softail cut a different profile than other Harley offerings. The Springer front fork used previously was supplanted by the Hydra-Glide models.

◆ While having the old school look, the new forks were designed with the latest CAD software.
◆ The Softail design meant the rear end rode on suspension that was hidden in the lower frame.
◆ 1,356 FXSTS Anniversary models were assembled for 1988.

The Springer fork also carried a front fender that rode 2 inches above the spoked wheel. Later versions would see the fender ride closer to the rubber.

As was typically the case, anniversary models were always decorated with special graphics to mark the occasion. Other badges would join the fuel tank appliquès.

1989 MODEL FLSTC
HERITAGE SOFTAIL CUSTOM

The FLSTC, or Heritage Softail Custom, was offered up in a special Super Bowl 23 edition. Fuel tank graphics were teamed up with a set of white saddlebags and matching saddle.

Owner: Harley-Davidson Archives

POLICE

1989 MODEL FXRP

Harley-Davidsons had a long history with their machines being used by law enforcement agencies. The FXRP was the latest entry into the market, and was seen on the streets of many cities both large and small.

◆ **Purpose-built for law enforcement, these "Police Specials" wore certified speedometers to accurately pace those exceeding posted speed limits.**

◆ **A solo saddle was also installed for the officer's comfort on the FXRP.**

◆ **780 of the 1989 FXRPs were assembled.**

Owner: Elmhurst Police Department

What law enforcement vehicle would be complete without at least one set of red and blue warning lights? This set resides at the front end of the FXRP, and strobe brightly when prompted.

A second, two-sided strobe was mounted atop the rear radio box. A third warning light was seen on a tall mast for better visibility.

1990 MODEL FLSTF FAT BOY

The FLSTF was named the "Fat Boy," and sported a new combination of features. The solid wheels at both ends and the monochromatic silver finish made this new model really stand out.

◆ 16-inch wheels were used at both ends of the new FLSTF.

◆ New 40mm Keihn carburetors were installed on every 1990 Harley.

◆ The Fat Boy was an instant success, and 4,440 copies were built in the first year of production.

Owner: Harley-Davidson Archives

The 80-cubic inch motor was accented by two of the seven stripes used on the new model, and was cradled in a frame that was painted in silver to complement the balance of the sheet metal.

1991 MODEL FXDB STURGIS

First sold for the 1980 model year, the Sturgis edition of the FXDB model resurfaced in 1991. While other 1991 FX models featured a set of three rubber motor mounts, the freshly designed chassis of the FXDB only required two.

◆ **The new frame design also resulted in several alterations to the motor for 1991.**
◆ **A 4-degree angle for motor mounting delivered a new geometry for the FXDB.**
◆ **A total of 1,546 Sturgis edition FXDB models were built for 1991.**

Owner: Ted Moran

The all-black motif of the Sturgis edition was carried over to every component on the FXDB. The glossy black transfer case was highlighted by a bright red stripe, and contained one of the two rubber drive train belts.

Each of the FXDB's cast wheels were finished in black and wore the complementary red accent stripe used throughout the machine.

1992 MODEL FXDB DAYTONA

Having already done two versions of a Sturgis FXDB, it was only fitting for H-D to have a model to commemorate 50 years of Daytona Beach's Bike Week. Special paint and graphics set the limited edition model apart from the other offerings from Harley that year.

◆ Both cast wheels and the rear belt drive socket were treated to a gold finish.

◆ Gold Pearlglo paint was offset by Indigo blue metallic.

◆ 1,700 Daytona FXDBs were created, keeping demand high and supply low.

Owner: Kersting's Harley-Davidson

Daytona Beach, Florida, had been the home for the official Bike Week celebration for 50 years in 1991, so Harley decided to build a bike to commemorate the occasion.

1993 MODEL FLSTN
HERITAGE "COW GLIDE"

Very few changes were made to the Softail models for 1993, but a new version of the Heritage was introduced. The "Cow Glide" was the result of adding black and white inserts of cattle pelts to the seat and saddlebags. The balance of the machine was also finished in black and white paint to complete the theme.

◆ 1993 was also Harley-Davidson's 90th year of production, and anniversary trimmed models were available to the public.

◆ Low-profile brake and clutch levers were added to the Softail lineup in 1993.

◆ Production for the FX and ST models topped 49,000 for the year.

Owner: Claudio Rauzi

Vast quantities of chrome were on hand to contrast with the black and white bovine theme on the FLSTN "Cow Glide" models in 1993.

1994 MODEL FLHTCU

For riders who preferred their journeys to be a bit longer, the chosen mount was often the big touring models. Harley's catalog for 1994 found the FLHTCU at the top of the list. Providing comfort and convenience, this "bagger" had it all.

◆ **FLHTCU rider and passenger were protected by a full coverage fairing, complete with lowers to keep wind and rain off of their boots and pants.**

◆ **"Ultra Classic" badges told the rest of the world you were aboard the best that Harley had to offer.**

◆ **Chrome case guards were among the shiny bits used to add some sparkle to the big machine.**

Owner: Heritage Harley-Davidson

With saddles fit for king and queen, the FLHTCU lacked nothing in creature comforts. The spacious saddlebags and rear storage box provided ample capacity for a weekend getaway.

Harley's 80-cubic inch V-twin motor powered the FLHTCU with plenty of torque and horsepower, regardless of payload.

1995 MODEL VR-1000

With hopes of racking up victories on the road race circuits, Harley introduced the VR-1000. Powered by a liquid-cooled V-twin, it was far removed from the standard Harley fare. While never reaching the levels of success H-D had hoped for, the VR-1000 made a perfect platform to develop the motor that eventually went into the V-Rod.

Owner: Harley-Davidson Archives

1995 MODEL FXSTSB BAD BOY

The Bad Boy was a new iteration to the Dyna family. Officially known as the FXSTSB, the new model was dipped in black and accessorized with chrome. The forward controls were factory installed for the long, lean riding position many riders favored.

◆ A laced front wheel was joined by a slotted disc at the rear.
◆ A set of shortened and staggered exhaust pipes handled the spent gases.
◆ The blacked-out springer fork provided comfort and style.

Owner: Heritage Harley-Davidson

The Bad Boy's slotted rear disc wheel was mated with a drilled brake rotor. As with all Softail models, the rear suspension was hidden between the lower frame rails. The result is a Softail ride with the look of a hard tail.

1997 MODEL FLSTS OL' BOY

Another variation on the Softail theme was the all-new Heritage Springer. Nicknamed the Ol' Boy due to its vintage bodywork and trim, it was another instant classic. From the fullness of the front fender to the detailed pillion and saddlebags, it took a sharp eye to realize this wasn't a Harley from the 1940s.

◆ The jeweled saddlebags were standard equipment, but there were plenty of options to go around.
◆ First-year FLSTS models were white with a choice of red or blue striping.
◆ Classic spoked wheels were wrapped with wide whitewall tires to complete the vintage look.

Owner: Kersting's Harley-Davidson

1997 MODEL FLSTF FAT BOY

A new kid on the block in 1990, the Fat Boy remained one of Harley's best sellers in 1997. It was no longer finished in the silver and yellow scheme, and each year featured a different set of hues. The twin set of solid disc wheels would become a trademark of the Fat Boy.

1997 MODEL FLSTC
HERITAGE SOFTAIL CLASSIC

The popularity of the Softail chassis was obvious by the many variations built on the design. The Heritage Softail Classic was the culmination of timeless design elements and modern technology. From the hydraulic front forks to the highly decorated leather saddlebags, there was plenty of eye candy for the serious rider.

◆ **The touring FL class of Harleys had bikes that all included overhead-valve twin-cylinder 80-cubic inch motors and five-speed transmissions.**

◆ **More than 30,000 big touring bikes, which included the FLSTC and nine other models, left the factory for 1997.**

◆ **Harley's lineup had grown to 22 models by 1997.**

Owner: Heritage Harley-Davidson

1998 MODEL XL1200S SPORTSTER

The Sportster is typically marketed to the beginning rider who wants a smaller machine, but still wants a Harley. Power was not their first priority. For those who wanted a Sportster AND power, the XL1200S was created. The 1200cc motor was fitted with a new cam and new twin plug cylinder heads. A higher 10:1 compression ratio also helped to boost the XL1200S rating by 7 more ponies.

◆ **The XL1200S was one of five different Sportster models sold in 1998.**
◆ **Weighing in at 501 lbs. dry, the bike had a 28-inch seat height that was perfect for shorter riders.**
◆ **The staggered shorty exhaust pipes were whisper quiet from the factory.**

A pair of easy-to-read instruments were aboard to monitor speed and rpms, as were a bank of indicator lights. To slow the fast XL200S, a trio of floating disc brakes were mounted to the cast-aluminum wheels. Vivid Black was the only color offered on the X1200S.

1998 MODEL FLSTS OL' BOY

The Ol' Boy returned for another year of robust sales in 1998, this time wearing a darker suit. The '98 models were sold in Vivid Black with a choice of red or blue trim. Being the 95th Anniversary year for Harley-Davidson, the Midnight Red with Champagne Pearl motif was also a choice for buyers.

Owner: Wheels Through Time Museum

1998 XL1200C SPORTSTER

For the Sportster buyer who wanted more flash than dash, the XL1200C was the way to go. In contrast to the newly released XL200S model, the Custom came with a plush saddle, higher bars, and added bits of chrome.

◆ The Sport and Custom had 1200cc motors built on the same platform.
◆ The Sport version included performance modifications in place of chrome.
◆ The XL1200C could be had with an optional Midnight Red and Champagne Pearl 95th anniversary paint scheme.

Owner: Wheels Through Time Museum

1999 MODEL FLHRI ROAD KING

Many, but not all, of the 1999 Harley-Davidsons received the new power plant from the factory. The new Twin-Cam 88 motor embodied the latest in technological advances, and some were even fed with fuel injection.

◆ A new football-shaped air cleaner was added to most of the Twin-Cam 88s, and made for obvious identification.
◆ The Road King was first seen as a 1994 model and served the needs of mid-range riders.
◆ Subtle enhancements and the new motor made the '99 Road King the best to date.

1999 MODEL FXSTB NIGHT TRAIN

Never willing to rest on its laurels when it came to introducing new models, Harley debuted the Night Train for 1999. Finished in three different types of black, this new Softail took darkness to a new level.

◆ The Night Train was driven by the new Twin Cam 88 motor, nicknamed the Fathead.
◆ The only things not done in black were the forks, exhaust and wheels.
◆ Based on the Softail chassis, the smooth-riding Night Train only looked uncomfortable.

Owner: Illinois Harley-Davidson

With the exception of the pushrod tubes and exhaust, the Night Train motor was devoid of chrome. Even the cooling fins were draped in black.

Most of the motor's cases were finished in wrinkle black paint—one of three types of black used on the Night Train. The bright fasteners are the only ray of light on the transfer case.

2000 MODEL FXSTD DEUCE

The improved FX frame made a home for the latest Softail member, the Deuce. The new chassis claimed a 34 percent increase in stiffness, and the new Fathead motor was bolted in for a new level of power. The stretched fuel tank and straight line rear fender added unique touches to the overall blend.

◆ **The rear tire was 17 inches in diameter and was stretched around a freshly minted solid rear disc wheel.**
◆ **Two-tone paint schemes were the order of the day on the Deuce.**
◆ **A staggered set of dual exhausts were a Deuce trademark.**

2001 MODEL FLTR ROAD GLIDE

Product placement for the Road Glides fell somewhere in between the Road King and ElectraGlide, and served both markets well. The frame-mounted fairing helped keep the rider in a quiet zone, and the hard-sided saddlebags kept gear dry and safe.

◆ **The 2001 FLTR wore a black headlight bezel—one of the minor changes for the year.**
◆ **An improved sound system was also included in the Road Glide's fairing for the new year.**
◆ **Cruise control, previously an option, was now standard equipment.**

2001 MODEL FLTR SCREAMING EAGLE

Regardless of how much comfort and convenience the FLTR offered, there were still some buyers who demanded a higher level of performance, too. For them, the Screaming Eagle version of the FLTR filled the bill. An extra 100 cc's of displacement was combined with floating-rotor brakes and special wheels. The Screaming Eagle graphics were hard to miss.

Owner: Walters Brothers Harley-Davidson

Behind the frame-mounted fairing of the Screaming Eagle FLTR is a set of white-faced gauges and the same upgraded sound system used on the standard FLTR.

2002 MODEL FXSTB NIGHT TRAIN

The first Night Train models were sold in 1999, and the blacked-out Softail remained a popular choice for Harley buyers. Powered by the latest in Harley-Davidson power plant technology, the motor was also trimmed with a liberal application of crinkle-black paint. Factory-delivered forward controls and Wide Glide forks completed the ensemble.

◆ **The 88-cubic inch motor had five speeds to choose from.**
◆ **The transfer case, oil tank and air cleaner were all treated to a layer of black wrinkle finish.**
◆ **A solid rear wheel was joined by a laced rim up front.**

Owner: Walters Brothers Harley-Davidson

The polished cooling fins of the motor contrast nicely against the all-black motif of the Night Train. Chrome-plated pushrod tubes and exhaust are also used to break up the monochromatic scheme used on the rest of the FXSTB.

2002 MODEL FXDWG 3

Harley-Davidson has attempted to build and sell a few "factory customs" through the years, but none have reached the level of the FXDWG 3. From the bikini and chin fairings to the custom upholstery on the seat, no inch of this machine has been overlooked. Custom paint completes the scene.

◆ **A set of five-spoke wheels was applied to this model only.**
◆ **Mirror stalks, grips and forward controls were also all specific to the FXDWG 3.**
◆ **Engraved identification logos abound so that no one mistakes this for a hand-built special.**

Owner: Walters Brothers Harley-Davidson

2002 MODEL XL-883R

With the look of the venerable XR-750, the 2002 Sportster was complete with several performance components behind the graphics and paint. The black wrinkle paint on the motor was offset by polished heads, and the exhaust was specifically created to aid in smooth flow of the exiting gases.

◆ Harley's successful racing heritage is reflected in the black, orange and checkerboard design.
◆ Cast wheels and a trio of disc brakes deliver looks and stopping power.
◆ The deeply stepped saddle makes a comfortable perch.

Owner: Walters Brothers Harley-Davidson

2002 MODEL VRSCA

Harley-Davidson threw its heritage to the wind when it decided to build the V-Rod. Although still powered by a V-twin motor, it was liquid cooled, something Harley had never put into production before. Using completely new hardware, and designing from scratch, the V-Rod builders reached new levels for factory performance.

◆ The 67.5-inch wheelbase was the longest of any bike produced by The Motor Company.
◆ With 11.3:1 compression, the factory motor produced 115 horsepower, another first for anything from the hallowed halls of Harley-Davidson.
◆ The V-Rod's fuel was stored in a tank that resided beneath the seat, lowering the center of gravity, and allowing more flexibility in the visible "fuel tank."

Owner: Harley-Davidson Motor Company

The liquid-cooled V-twin was like nothing Harley had ever built before. It delivers power and smoothness at levels only dreamed of in previous machinery from The Motor Company.

2003 MODEL FXSTD 100TH ANNIVERSARY SOFTAIL DEUCE

With 100 years of building motorcycles under their belt it was time to celebrate. The 100th anniversary models came complete with a raft of badges and special paint. The Softail Deuce was still among the living, and wore the appropriate birthday suit.

Owner: Heritage Harley-Davidson

The Fathead motor was still being employed, and the Deuce had black jugs with polished fins. Bright cylinder heads added to the sparkle.

Several different applications of anniversary trim were used on the air cleaners of the 2003 models, and the FXSTD model featured an all-chrome finish with a centrally mounted birthday badge.

The official anniversary badges were applied to every 2003 Harley-Davidson, and the fuel tank was home for the largest of them.

2004 BUELL XB12R

While hardly a traditional Harley-Davidson, the Buell line is sold on the same showroom floor as the rest of the Harley models. The Buell brand is owned by The Motor Company and powered by motors from the Sportster catalog, so the lineage is undeniable. Created for the rider who demands top performance from his two-wheeled crafts, the XB12R meets and exceeds those needs.

◆ The 1203cc, V-twin motor is fed with 49mm downdraft fuel injection.

◆ A dry weight of only 395 lbs. provides the pilot with a machine that responds instantly.

◆ Racing Red paint is paired with gold anodized wheels for a truly unique look.

Owner: Heritage Harley-Davidson

One of the best innovations on the XB12R is the fuel-in-frame design. The molded cover above the alloy frame simply hides electronics, while the actual fuel is stored within the walls of the frame.

While the fuel is carried in the frame, the XB12R's oil is held within the swingarm casting. Eric Buell has a longstanding reputation for ingenuity, and the current lineup is proof of his design capability.

2004 MODEL FLSTF FAT BOY

Immediately after being released for the 1990 model year, the Fat Boy earned high marks from the buying public. 2004 would see the FLSTF back for another year, with only minimal changes. The full metal fenders, massive floorboards and solid disc wheels remained unchanged.

Owner: Heritage Harley-Davidson

2004 MODEL VRSCA

The first editions of the V-Rod were trimmed in silver bodywork and a silver frame. While this was distinctive, many potential buyers wanted some color in their lives. For 2004, a variety of hues were offered on the silver-framed VRSCA, including Vivid Black, Impact Blue, Lava Red Sunglo, as well as a pair of two-tone options.

Owner: Heritage Harley-Davidson

2004 MODEL VRSCB

Not a company willing to leave well enough alone, Harley-Davidson added the VRSCB to the V-Rod family tree in 2004. The VRSCB rolled with a chassis dipped in black, and the power train is a combination of black and polished alloy. An altered final drive ratio, high-efficiency valve heads, and an improved fuel gauge rounded out the changes for the entire lineup of V-Rods.

Owner: Heritage Harley-Davidson

2005 MODEL FLSTN DELUXE

Joining the ever-expanding Softail family in 2005 is the Deluxe. The combination of full fenders, available two-tone paint and vintage badging harkens back to the classic days of Harley-Davidson.

◆ **The latest twin-cam 88B motor provides the Deluxe with plenty of modern power, and can be fed with a choice of carburetor or fuel injection.**

◆ **Every Softail machine built for 2005 will sport a new headlight housing, and the face of the lamp will bear the Bar & Shield logo.**

◆ **A new Profile Laced wheel design mounts to the rubber without the typical lip at the wheel's edge.**

Owner: Heritage Harley-Davidson

The new Deluxe is full of new design features, and the winged tank badge is one of them.

The new Softail headlight housing and lamp are flanked by a pair of classic driving lights on this Deluxe, bringing back the look of the first "Glide" models.

2005 MODEL FLSTC SPRINGER CLASSIC

Another new entrant in the 2005 catalog is the Softail Springer Classic. From the Springer front fork to the super-wide beach bars, the new Classic screams "old school." A pair of roomy floorboards only adds to the nostalgic appeal of the latest step back in time.

◆ **The Springer Classic can be ordered with either carburetor or fuel injection, but either way the twin-cam 88B is in the house.**

◆ **A low 25.9-inch saddle height makes the Classic accessible to nearly every rider.**

◆ **A selection of solid or two-tone paint options await the Classic buyer.**

Owner: Heritage Harley-Davidson

Along with the trimmed saddlebags and old school front fender, the hub has been adorned with a teardrop-shaped chrome trim piece.

The fuel tank on the Springer Classic is divided by a chrome strip, much like the 1940s models. The teardrop badge fits nicely with the vintage theme.

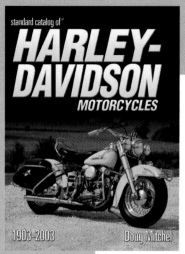